CHILDREN PRAYING

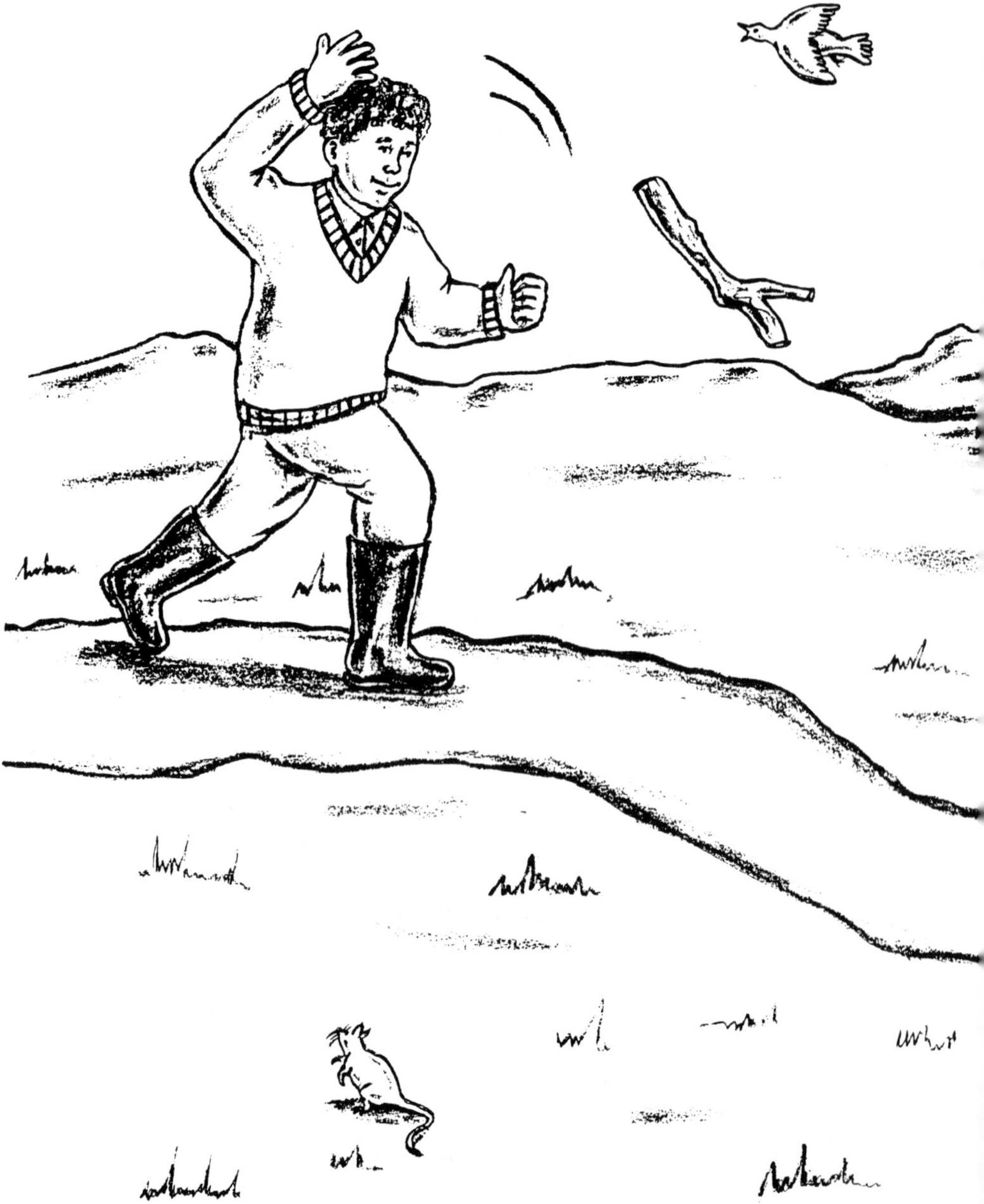

Children Praying

With Illustrations by
JACQUELINE STEVENSON

SAINT ANDREW PRESS

First published in 1991 by
SAINT ANDREW PRESS
121 George Street, Edinburgh EH2 4YN

Translated from the Gaelic edition – *Clann ag Urnaigh* – which was published on behalf of the PANEL on WORSHIP of the CHURCH of SCOTLAND

Copyright © the PANEL on WORSHIP of
the CHURCH of SCOTLAND 1991

ISBN 0 7152 0659 1

All rights reserved. No part of this publication may be reproduced or transmitted in any form or by any means, electronic or mechanical, including photocopy, recording, or information storage and retrieval system, without permission in writing from the publisher. This book is sold, subject to the condition that it shall not, by way of trade or otherwise, be lent, re-sold, hired out or otherwise circulated without the publisher's prior consent.

> **British Library Cataloguing in Publication Data**
> A catalogue record for this
> book is available from the
> British Library
>
> ISBN 0 7152 0659 1

This book has been set in 14/16 Garamond.
Illustrations by Jacqueline Stevenson.
Book design by Mark Blackadder.

Printed and bound by Bell and Bain Ltd, Glasgow

Contents

Part I
Morning and evening prayers for
each day of the week   1

Part II
Prayers for special occasions   17

Part III
Graces   29

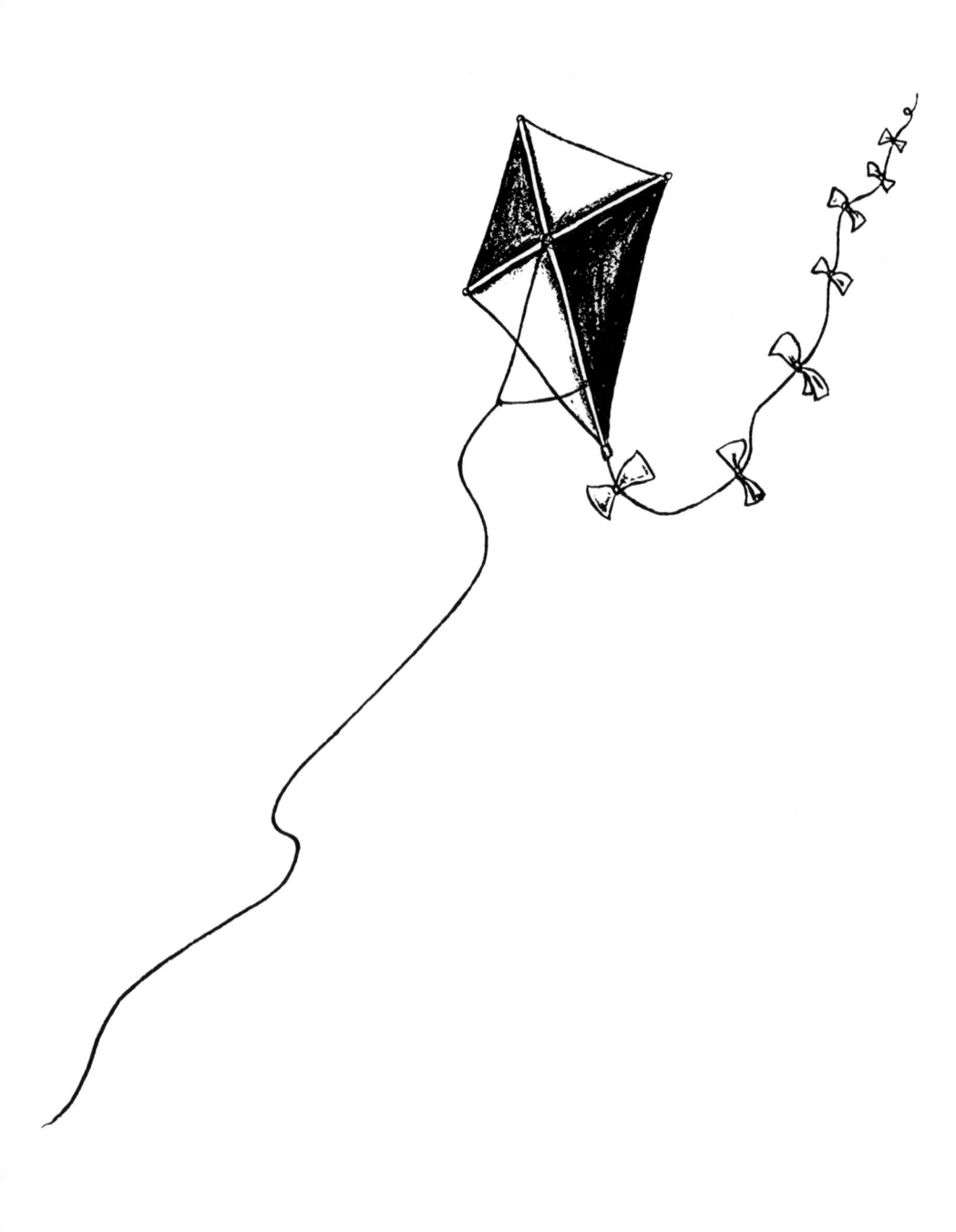

INTRODUCTION

Children Praying is the English edition of the Church of Scotland Panel on Worship's Gaelic book for children – *Clann ag Urnaigh*.

The aim of this book is to encourage faith in children and to provide prayers suitable for use in the context of family worship, in playgroups, schools and within Churches. If the use of this book goes beyond the devotional into the whole field of education, nothing would please the authors more.

The Saint Andrew Press is grateful to the Panel on Worship and to all who worked together towards the original Gaelic publication and this English translation.

Adapted from Norman Maciver's Introduction to
Clann ag Urnaigh
Aberdeen 1991

PART I

Morning and evening prayers for each day of the week

SUNDAY

Morning

All I desire is personal knowledge of Christ and of the power which comes from his resurrection. (Philippians 3:10)

Gracious God,
Today your children remember with thankfulness the resurrection of your son, Jesus Christ. I am glad that he is with me, surrounding me with his love. Strengthen me to follow Jesus without shame. Amen

The Lord's Prayer

SUNDAY

Evening

And when evening came that same day, on the first day of the week . . . . Jesus came and stood in the midst and said "Peace be to you". (St John 20:19)

Thank you, Father, that Jesus, your Son, lives, and that he is with me now, nearer than hand or foot, closer than my breath. Lord Jesus, I have faith and therefore am not afraid. Let me be at peace all night long. For Jesus sake.   Amen

MONDAY

Morning

Then said Jesus to them again "Peace be unto you. As the Father has sent me so send I you". (St John 20:21)

Lord send me forth today with your peace:
Where there is hatred, planting love,
Where there is injury, mercy;
Where there is strife, reconciliation;
Where there is doubt, faith;
Where there is despair, courage;
Where there is darkness, light;
Where there is sorrow, joy.   Amen

MONDAY

Evening

Keep me as the apple of the eye, under the shade of your wings hide me. (PSALM 17:8)

Lord, grant that I may give comfort rather than
   seek comfort.
That I may be ready to hear rather than be
   heard.
For it is in self-denial that we find ourselves,
In being merciful that we receive mercy.
And in dying we are born into life eternal.
                                      Amen

TUESDAY

Morning

As the Father has loved me so have I loved you. (St John 15:9)

The sun has risen, giving us a new day.
Lord, shed the light of your love in my heart;
Love to my companions,
Love to my enemies,
Love to all,
Kindly love, fearless love,
Jesus, your Son's love to me,
Your love to him,
Love which lasts forever.　　　　　　Amen

TUESDAY

Evening

Behold the keeper of Israel neither slumbers nor sleeps.
(PSALM 121:4)

God my heavenly Father, though I am tired and sleepy, your love is tireless and unsleeping. In my sleep keep me safe. Watch over those who must remain awake to help and comfort others.

Amen

WEDNESDAY

Morning

Consider how the lilies grow in the field; they toil not and spin not. Yet I tell you, even Solomon in all his glory was not clothed like one of them. (St Matthew 6:28 and 29)

Thank you, O God, for my awakening and the power to rise. As I put clothing on my body, may you put the shade of your mercy over my soul. And as the warmth of the sun lifts the mist from the hills, lift the mist of my doubts with the warmth of your love.   Amen

WEDNESDAY

Evening

I write to you, little children, because your sins are forgiven. (1 JOHN 2:12)

O Jesus without sin, King of heaven and earth, Saviour of the world, surround us tonight with your love: . . . . (brother, sister, father, mother, grandparents). Thank you for my home with its warmth, food and clothing. Bless those I love and your children everywhere. Create in me a clean heart, O God.   Amen

THURSDAY

Morning

By this shall all know that you are my disciples if you love one another. (St John 13:35)

O God, I am so glad that you love all. That means that you love me. You love me when we play, and when my companions and I are on good terms and helping each other. You did not stop loving me the day I was cross and impatient. Give me the heart that Jesus had, who gave gladness to every one he met.   Amen

THURSDAY

Evening

Come to me all you who labour and are heavy laden, and I will give you rest. (St Matthew 11:28)

O God, full of love, hear my prayer.
If we have done things which shame us, show
   us the right way.
Thank you that the love which surrounded us
   all day goes with us into the peace of night.
Amen

FRIDAY

Morning

Ask and you will receive; seek and you will find.
(St Matthew 7:7)

Gracious Father, it is not easy for me to pray or to find words. You know my thoughts, and I know that you love me. In your love, you will give me all I need. You will keep from me things I ask which would do me harm. In your love you refuse. In your love you give. Your love is wonderful. Teach me your will.   Amen

FRIDAY

Evening

And lo, I am with you always to the end of the world.
(St Matthew 28:20)

The sun is setting. Night comes on. Flowers are closing. All birds and animals return home.

O Jesus, give to all who are tired tonight the rest and blessing of your love. Be near those who suffer. Protect those who travel by car, train, ship, or plane. Guide them safely homeward.

Forgive my sins. Give me peace of mind and quiet sleep. Amen

SATURDAY

Morning

Jesus rejoiced in spirit and said "I thank you, O Father, Lord of heaven and earth, that you have hidden these things from the wise and understanding and revealed them to babes." (St Luke 10:21)

O God, our Father in heaven,
give me health for my body
        health for my mind
        health for my soul.

I come to you, seeking strength to be better today than I was yesterday. Show me your will in thought, word, and deed.   Amen

SATURDAY

Evening

Blessed and honoured be our God
Who ever on us pours
His gifts. He is our health
Who daily life restores. (PSALM 68:19)

Heavenly Father, thank you for the freedom and happiness of today. I am safe in your hand tonight. Prepare us to praise you together tomorrow, your holy day, the joyful day of resurrection.
Amen

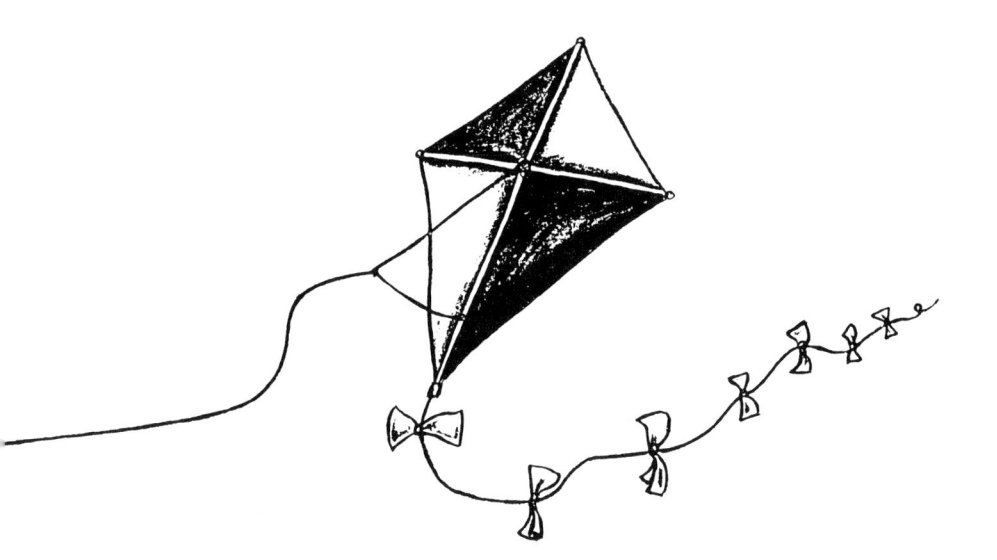

PART II
Prayers for special occasions

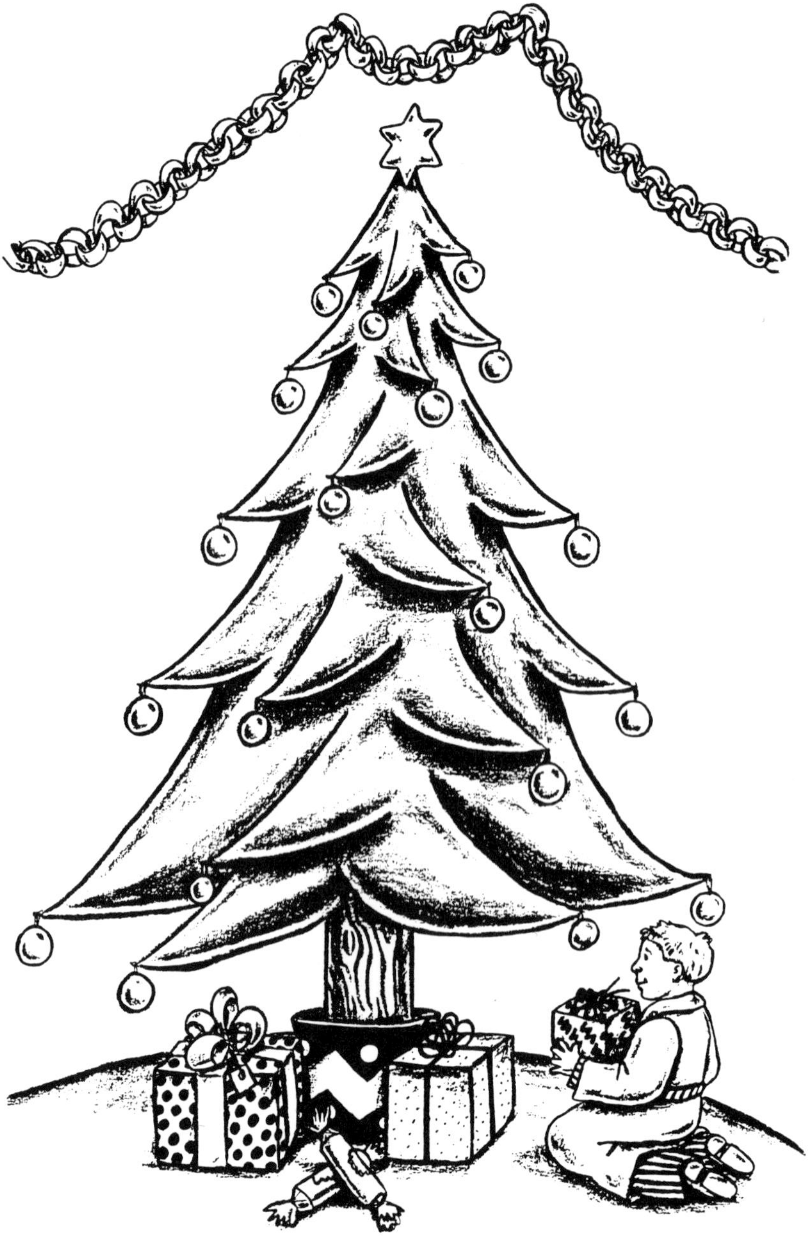

CHRISTMAS

We thank you, God, for Christmas-time,
for the joyful hymns we sing,
for the parties we have,
for services in school
and church,
for the gifts we receive
and give.

When we receive a gift may we remember Christ, the gift you gave at the first Christmas. When we see lights on the Christmas trees and in the streets may we remember that Jesus is the Light of the World. When we hear about Jesus who was born in a stable, may we remember those who have neither food nor homes nor friends.

                                                            Amen

EASTER

We thank you, God, for the things that happened at Easter time:
Friday, when Christ was crucified for us;
The Sabbath, when he came back from the dead.
Thank you for the power we see in his resurrection from the dead.

Help us to see the blessings we have because Jesus rose again. Fill us with joy for the benefits we have received because of Christ who is alive and with us every day.
Amen

HOLIDAYS

Thank you, God, that the holidays have come,
when we have a rest from school work,
when we play in the park,
on the shore, in the woods,
when we visit other places,
when we see new things,
when we meet new friends,
when we visit our relatives.

Help us to get pleasure from the beauty of the world during the sunny years of summer. May we remember those, old and young, who are confined to their homes or are in hospital while we are playing outside.

                                                   Amen

HARVEST

Thank you, God, for the fruits of the earth,
for the work of crofters and farmers,
Thank you for the harvest of the sea,
for the work of fishermen.
Thank you for everything that grows on the earth,
trees, plants, flowers;
for the precious things we get in the ground:
peat, coal.
Thank you for the blessings that come from the ocean:
white fish and shellfish, oil and gas.

Help us to make use of the things we get; and may we remember those in this country and in other lands who do not possess the blessings we have.
                                              Amen

A NEW BABY

Father in heaven we give thanks for the small baby you have given us. We were so happy when he/she came home from hospital along with Mummy. He/she is so bonny and we love him/her. Help us to take care of our new baby. Keep him/her safe all his/her life – and our whole family.

Amen

DEATH OF A GRANDMOTHER

O God, I was weeping for a long time when Granny died, for I loved her very much and I miss her. But I know she is with Christ in heaven and that makes me happy. I pray that our whole family will one day be in heaven with Granny.

Amen

A BIRTHDAY

Lord, I know you have given us our life. Today I am so thankful for it. Give us joy in remembering the birthday of {insert name}. We love him/her very much. Today we shall play, eat, and laugh together. Bless us and keep us mindful that Jesus is with us.

Amen

ILLNESS – IN HOSPITAL

Jesus, on earth you went through the villages healing folk. [Insert name] is sick. Be with him/her. Heal him/her and strengthen him/her. Help the doctors so that someday soon he/she may get home. Thank you Jesus.

Amen

FIRST DAY AT SCHOOL

Heavenly Father, the day has arrived when I go to school. I am pleased, for I shall be with my new friends. But the school is so big, and Mummy will not be with me. But you said you would not leave me, and that helps. Be with me and with Mummy at home.

Amen

VISITORS – GRANNY

Lord, Granny comes today, and I hope she will stay a while. She is so good to me, and so kind. She is so generous. I am glad she is coming, for I love her very much. She sits with me, listening, speaking, and telling me of Jesus. Thank you that she is coming.

Amen

PART III

Graces

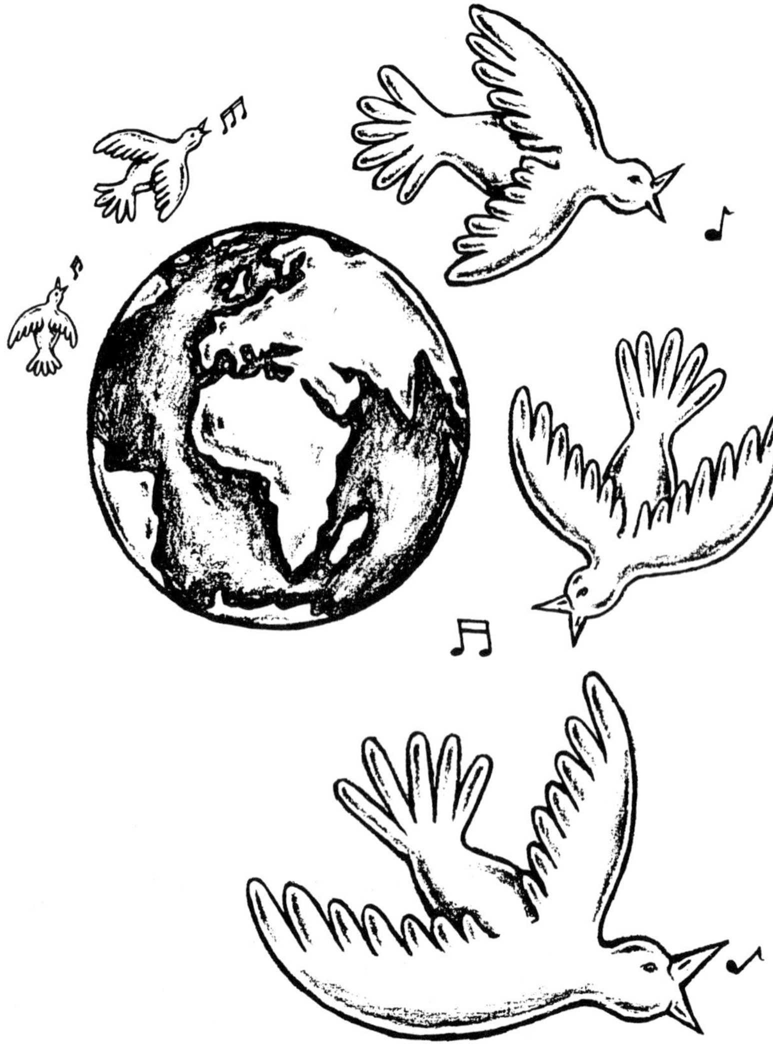

A GRACE FOR THE WORLD OF NATURE

Thank you for the beautiful world,
Thank you for drink and food,
Thank you for birds singing:
It is God who made all.

A GRACE FOR CREATION

From God all things flow
For us and all his creatures:
And so, with the angels above,
To the Holy Trinity we sing praise.

A FAMILY GRACE

Food and drink according to our need,
With gentle parents and friends:
All come down from God our Father –
To the Holy Trinity our lasting praise.

A GRACE FOR THE HUNGRY

Throughout the world many mouths are empty
Without drink or food:
O hasten the day when there shall be
No destitution on land or sea.

THE PSALMIST'S GRACE

The earth and its fulness belongs to God
For he made it;
Now thanks be to him since he gives us
Food according to our need.

A GRACE FOR LITTLE CHILDREN

Thanks to God, thanks to God,
In the morning thanks to God,
At table we offer thanks anew
And at bed-time may he close our eyes.

THE GRACE OF THE MIRACLES

Thank you for Jesus
Who came to set us free
And fed fainting people
With his miracles of love.

THE BARD'S GRACE

Some have food but no appetite;
Some are hungry without food;
But we have food and health;
May the Lord therefore be praised.

A CONTEMPORARY GRACE

For pictures on the "telly",
For bread, butter, and jam,
Mummy, Daddy, cat and dog,
And all the things I enjoy:
All night and all day
I will love my Heavenly Father.

GRACE FOR SUNDAY

Thanks to God for Sunday School
Where Jesus himself is present;
Thanks to God for the church
With joyous worship every week;
Thanks also be to him
Who gives us food according to our need.